This book
belongs to

Susie's Tale

Hand With Paw We Changed the Law

Susie's HOPE

by Donna Lawrence

illustrations and cover design by Jennifer Tipton Cappoen

Book and Cover Designer: Jennifer Tipton Cappoen
Copy Editor: Lynn Bemer Coble
Photographers: Erin Arsenault, Jerry Wofford

Published by **Paws and Claws Publishing, LLC**
1589 Skeet Club Road, Suite 102-175
High Point, NC 27265
www.PawsandClawsPublishing.com
info@pawsandclawspublishing.com

Susie's Books is an imprint of
Paws and Claws Publishing, LLC

1589 Skeet Club Road, Suite 102-175
High Point, NC 27265
www.PawsandClawsPublishing.com
info@pawsandclawspublishing.com

ISBN #978-0-9906067-1-0
Printed in the United States

Special Thanks...

I would like to thank my husband Roy and my family and friends for all of their support.

Thank you to everyone behind Susie's Law for all of their hard work and dedication.

A very special thank you to the wonderful people at the Guilford County Animal Shelter for saving Susie.

I also want to thank Roberta and Bob Wall for fostering Susie and for their help in nursing her back to health and in finding her a permanent home.

I would like to thank the man who found Susie in the park and cared enough to call for help.

I would also like to thank Ally Thomas with Southern Tails for all of the dog training that she has provided to Susie and me.

Most of all, I thank God for bringing Susie into my life at a time when I needed her the most.

~Donna Lawrence

This book is dedicated to all of the animals out there that had no voice but that now—thanks to Susie—have been given a voice.

Arise, shine; for thy light is come, and the glory of the Lord is risen upon thee.
Isaiah 60:1

Table of Contents

Susie's Tale 6

Hand With Paw We Changed

    the Law 42

Susie's Photo Album 44

Susie's Special Friends

    Phoenix and Deborah 48

    Bailey and Keely 50

The Susie's Hope™ Program Is 53

Susie's Hope™ Pledge 54

In Susie's Words 55

Susie's Trainer 56

Susie and Donna—Survivors 58

Forgiveness 59

Instrumental People 60

About the Author, Susie, and

    the Artist 62

My name is Susie. I was all alone in
a park in Greensboro, North Carolina. I
was only ten weeks old. My owner had hurt
me. I had a broken jaw, missing teeth, and open
sores from burns. I was really scared. I had no
food and no water. It was August. And it was
very hot.

Flies buzzed around me all of the time. My burns
itched and hurt. How I wanted to scratch them! When
I did, they hurt even more. Where my ears had been
there were just nubs.

I was afraid in the daytime. But it was at night when I got really scared. It was so dark, and there were a lot of strange noises. I hid under bushes and curled up to make myself really small. The shadows looked like monsters. I didn't want a wild animal to find me and eat me.

Every night I had nightmares. I would see my owner beating me and then burning me all over again. Then I'd wake up whimpering and sweating. I was scared to go back to sleep.

Day after day, I walked alone in the park. I was getting desperate. I knew that I needed to find food and water. I ate trash and sticks. My mouth hurt so much when I chewed. Each morning the hot sun and flies woke me up. Then I stretched, stood up, and hobbled along. I was getting closer and closer to dying. And I knew it. I was almost ready to give up.

One day my luck changed. A man was walking in the park. He saw me and stopped. He got down on one knee. His shocked eyes looked deeply into my big, brown eyes. Ever so gently, he picked me up. He held me close as he dialed his cell phone.

He hugged me gently and said, "Don't give up, little girl. Help is on the way. You're going to be all right." He made me feel safe.

11

Soon a truck pulled up. Someone got out, and the caring man in the park handed me to them. *Who was this person?* The person carefully set me in a cage in the back of the truck. Then we drove away. *Where were we going?* I really didn't care. I had nothing left in me. I was so tired that I fell asleep.

When we got to the animal shelter, someone new opened the side door of the truck. I was a little worried. I didn't know what they were going to do to me. They picked me up carefully. I didn't know where I was. And I didn't know any of these people. I was too worn out to care.

The veterinarian and vet techs all crowded around me. They looked shocked, angry, and worried. They carried me into the shelter. Everyone stared and whispered. They couldn't believe that someone had done this to me.

"Poor little puppy. She has a broken jaw and missing teeth. And she has second- and third-degree burns on most of her body. Her ears are almost gone. Who could have done this to her? Who could have hurt her like this? Poor baby."

They put me in the center of a table in a room that was very bright. Medical equipment was all around. It was shiny and silver and a little scary. I felt very small in the middle of that table. I knew that all eyes were on me. Everyone talked at once. They tried to figure out what to do first.

I wanted the veterinarian to know that I wouldn't give up. I looked straight into her eyes and licked her hand. She said, "This little girl is a fighter. And we're going to help her get better."

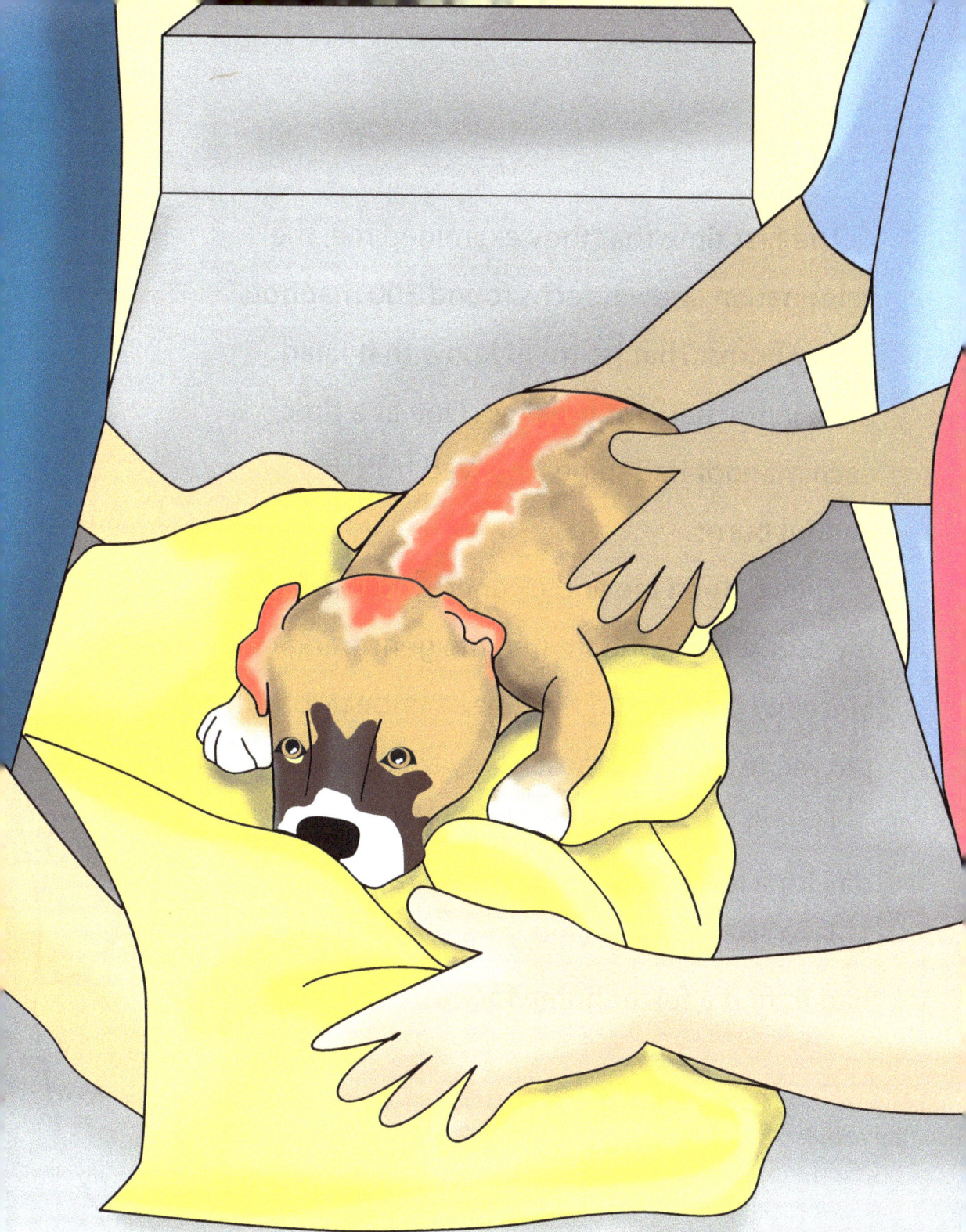

The first time that they examined me, the veterinarian and vet techs found 300 maggots on my burns. That let them know that I had been in the park for ten days. One at a time, each maggot had to be removed from my painful burns.

They bathed me and cleaned and bandaged my burns. Everyone treated me gently and carefully. Since my pain would have been unbearable, they put me to sleep for most of my treatments.

I needed lots of medical care every day for a long time. I could only stay at the animal shelter for a while. The staff there had to find a foster home for me.

Roberta and Bob Wall agreed to foster me. They brought me to their home. They already had three white, fluffy lapdogs and two cats. *Would their other pets accept me?* My foster parents took care of all of my special needs. They loved me and cared for me. They even gave me a room of my own.

My foster dad drove me to the Guilford County Animal Shelter for my medical treatments. The staff there did what my foster parents couldn't do at home. Each time the vet techs put me to sleep to spare me the pain. They cleaned my burns and changed the bandages. At first my foster dad took me every day. Then it was every other day.

At home my foster dad also took more maggots off my painful skin. He said that his stomach could take it. He became my hero.

My foster parents had a vacation planned. They couldn't take me, and I still needed lots of special care. That's when Donna Lawrence got to know me.

During their vacation, Donna came to their home every day. She spent lots of time with me in my special room. We watched movies and Donna rubbed my head.

Donna followed my foster parents' directions for medications and special care very closely. Like my foster dad, Donna drove me to the animal shelter for care that couldn't be done at home.

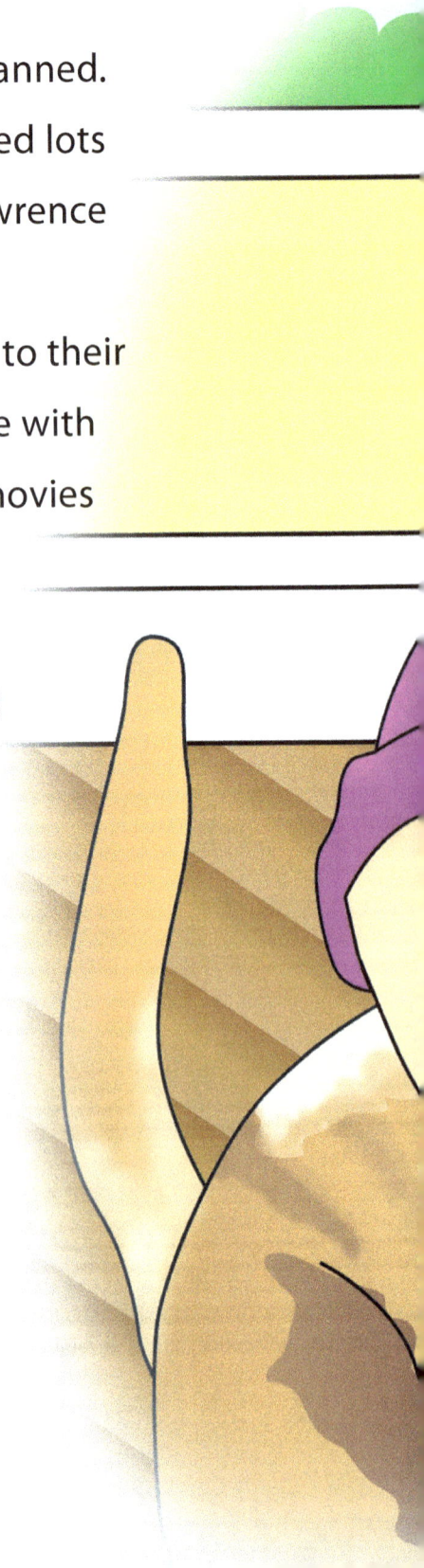

21

Roberta and Bob came back from vacation. They knew that it was time to find me a permanent home. I was almost fully grown…not a puppy anymore. They already had five other pets, and I was in their territory. *I needed my own family, place, and space.*

During the search for my permanent home, Donna Lawrence helped them out by taking me to her home on the weekends. At Donna's I got to lie around and relax in her fenced-in backyard. I loved chasing Donna's dog, Baby Girl, in the backyard. We ran and ran.

23

I was a shepherd–pit bull mix. That made it harder to place me in a home. A lot of people don't trust pit bulls. After the long search, Donna and her husband Roy decided to adopt me. They signed the adoption papers.

Then the moving day arrived. My foster parents unloaded my cage, toys, and clothes. I jumped on every piece of furniture in Donna and Roy's home. Then Baby Girl and I played like never before.

I was home. I had my own home and my own family. Donna and Roy had Baby Girl, seven cats, and me.

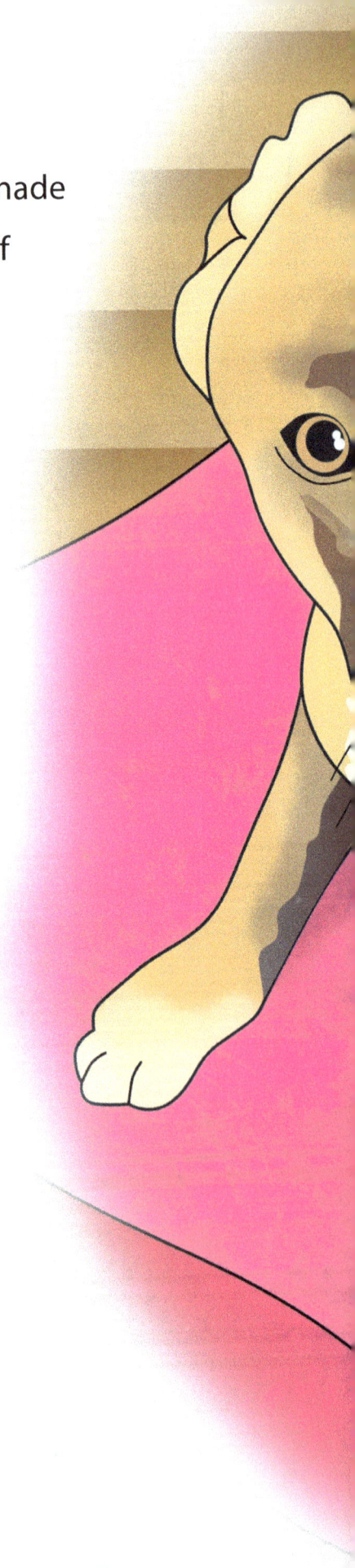

I moved into their home in December. My first Christmas with Donna, Roy, and Baby Girl was a special one. Donna had lots of costumes and toys as gifts for both of us dogs. We got gifts at home and at Donna's beauty salon, The Kutting Edge, in Greensboro.

One night as Baby Girl and I were playing, I growled. That growl terrified Donna. She didn't know what to think. The next morning I heard her call Roberta and Bob. She told them that she may have made a mistake. *I had to let Donna know that I was meant to be in her home.*

About a year before Donna met me, her neighbors moved. They couldn't take their pit bull with them. For five years, they had chained their dog outdoors, left it alone, and underfed it. Donna felt sorry for the dog. After they moved, she took food and water to the dog every morning.

One day when Donna was feeding the pit bull, it attacked her. It knocked her down and grabbed her right leg in its jaws. She kicked the dog off with her left leg. That made it more angry. It jumped for her throat. Donna held the dog in midair by its collar. It chewed on her hand.

She heard a voice say, "Throw and roll." That's what Donna did. She threw the dog off her and rolled out of its reach. Then she ran to a neighbor's home. He took her to the emergency room. There she got 45 stitches in her leg.

Donna walked with crutches. It took her months to walk again. When she went back to work, she sat on a stool to cut hair. She had never been scared of dogs. This attack made her afraid of them. Like Susie alone in the park, Donna had nightmares about her attack.

That dog's attack was why my growl while Baby Girl and I played terrified Donna.

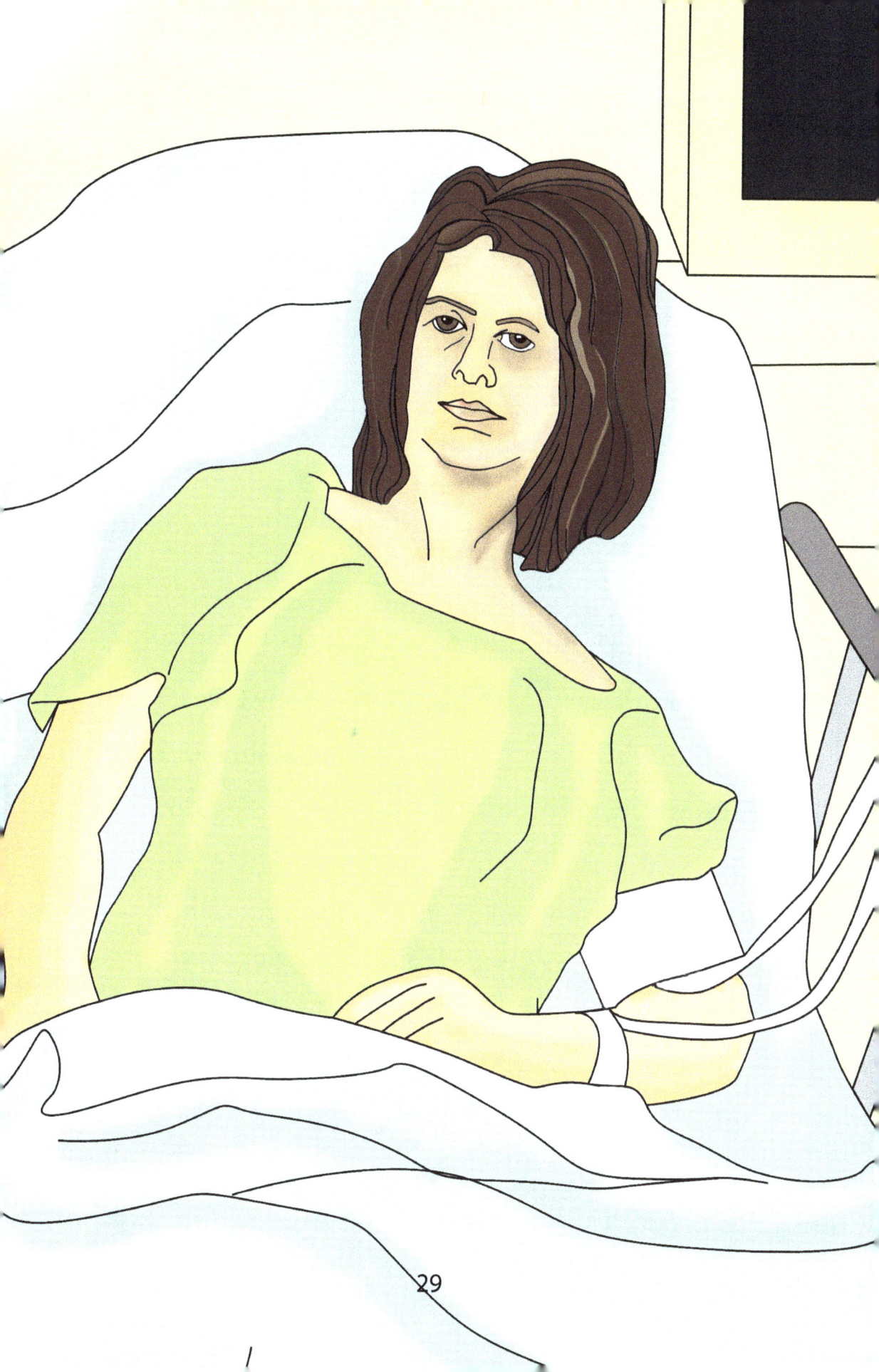

Roberta and Bob asked Donna and me to join them on a summer beach trip. That was my first trip to the beach. I ran on the beach and jumped in the waves. And I rolled in the sand. I ran and ran and ran.

Donna and I went out very early every morning that week. And she took lots of pictures. I loved the beach and the waves.

31

My mom and I have gone to schools, churches, and groups. My mom has shared our stories. We taught children how to take care of their pets. We also taught them how to be safe around animals. My mom and I showed the crowd the tricks I have learned.

We have started the Susie's Hope™ organization. Through it, we spread the message of love, hope, and forgiveness. We both survived attacks. We have taught each other to love and respect again.

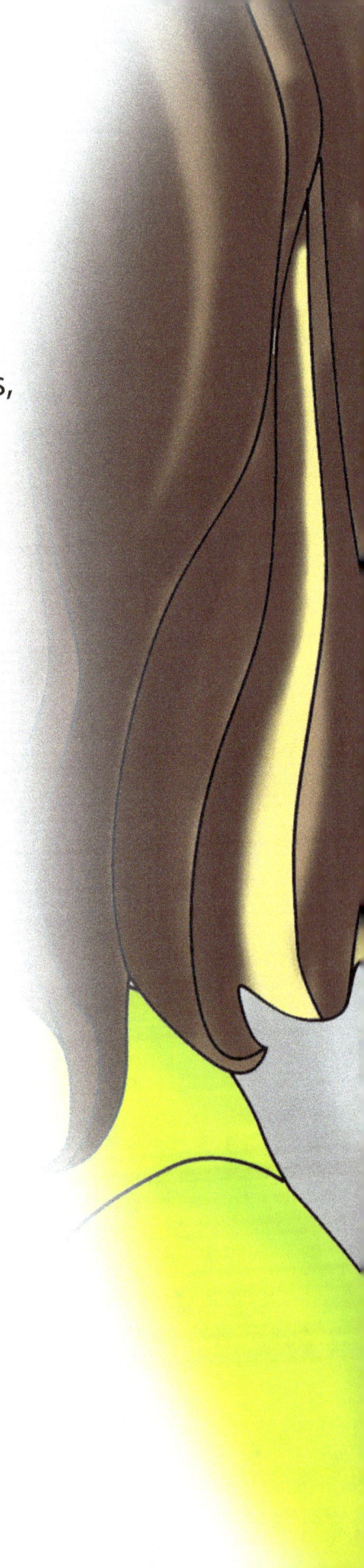

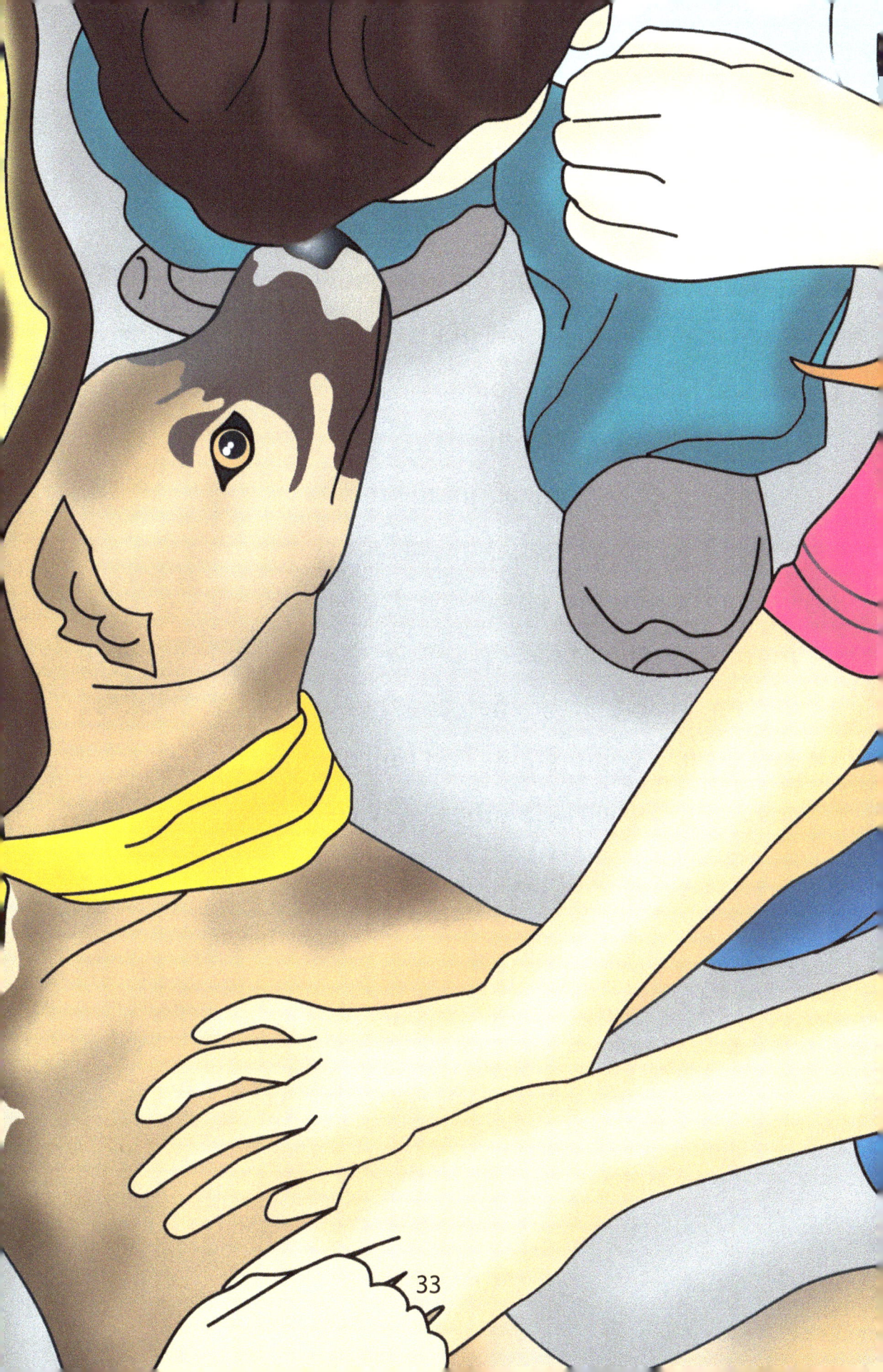

33

My trainer has taught my mom how to teach me to do tricks. My mom and I have worked hard on my training.

I have learned all of the basic commands. My mom taught me to ride a skateboard. She taught me to jump through hoops too. I have loved making my mom proud of me.

I am going to be trained as a therapy dog. I will visit burn units and cancer units in hospitals. I will help others survive.

My mom and I had our day in court. I had to face the man who hurt me. My mom and my foster mom had TV crews there. Many people came to be there for me. I slept by my mom. I looked at the man in the courtroom. He could not hurt me again. My mom could tell that I forgave him for what he did.

My foster dad walked me up to the judge. He wanted the judge to see how bad my burns were.

The lawyer asked everyone to stand up to support me. Half of the people there stood up. My mom was proud that so many people came to court.

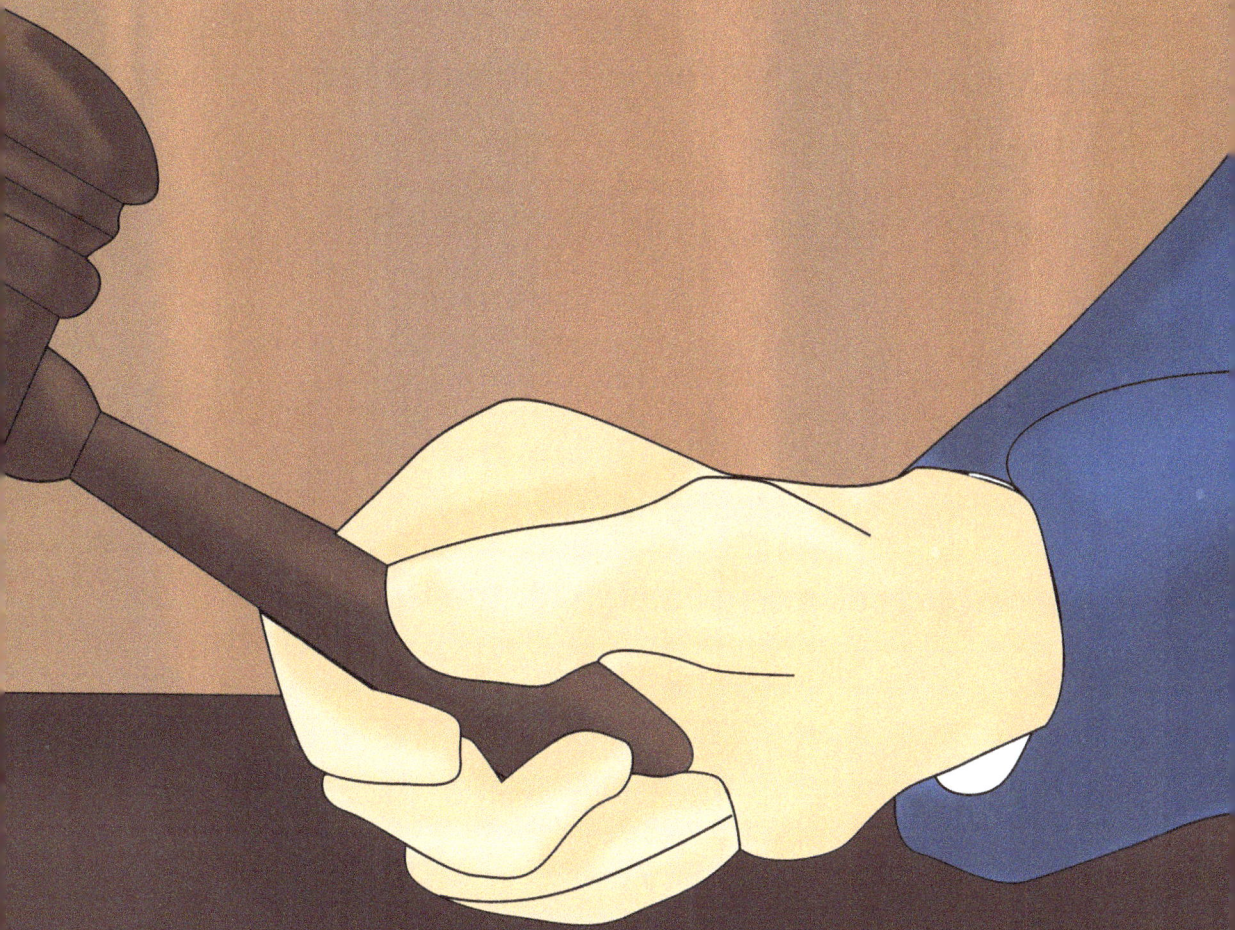

My mom, my foster mom, and many others wanted to make a new law. They wanted it to let a judge give jail time to people who have hurt animals. First they found out how the laws at that time worked.

Then they got many people to write letters and E-mails to our state representatives in Raleigh. North Carolina Senator Don Vaughan worked with us to change the law. He said to call it Susie's Law. I was excited about that.

My mom took me to Raleigh for the House session. She walked me around the room. Then they could see my scars. The bill passed with no one voting against it.

LEGI
BUI

39

In June 2010, my mom and I went to Raleigh to the governor's mansion. I had dressed up with my nails painted pink and my pearls around my neck. That was the first time I wore my pearls.

We met the governor before the bill was signed. We also met her two dogs. She hugged my mom. Then she shook my paw and rubbed my head.

The governor signed the bill in the backyard of the mansion. My mom and I were right beside her. My paw print is stamped on the bill. How cool is that!

Susie's Law went into effect in December 2010.

GEN[...]LINA

SENATE BILL 254
RATIFIED BILL

06-18-10A09:08 RCVD

AN ACT TO INCREASE THE PENALTY FOR THE MALICIOUS ABUSE, TORTURE, OR KILLING OF AN ANIMAL.

The General Assembly of North Carolina enacts:

SECTION 1. G.S. 14-360(a1) reads as rewritten:
"(a1) If any person shall maliciously kill, or cause or procure to be killed, any animal by intentional deprivation of necessary sustenance, that person shall be guilty of a ~~Class A1 misdemeanor.~~ Class H felony."

SECTION 2. G.S. 14-360(b) reads as rewritten:
"(b) If any person shall maliciously torture, mutilate, maim, cruelly beat, disfigure, poison, or kill, or cause or procure to be tortured, mutilated, maimed, cruelly beaten, disfigured, poisoned, or killed, any animal, every such offender shall for every such offense be guilty of a ~~Class I~~ Class H felony. However, nothing in this section shall be construed to increase the penalty for cockfighting provided for in G.S. 14-362."

SECTION 3. This act becomes effective December 1, 2010, and applies to offenses committed on or after that date.
In the General Assembly read three times and ratified this the 17th day of June, 2010.

_____
Walter H. Dalton
President of the Senate

_____
William L. Wainwright
Speaker Pro Tempore of the House of [...]

_____
Beverly E. Perdue
Governor

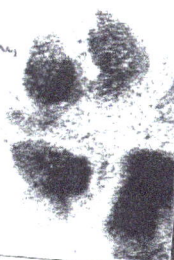

41

Hand With Paw

We Changed the Law

Susie's

Photo Album

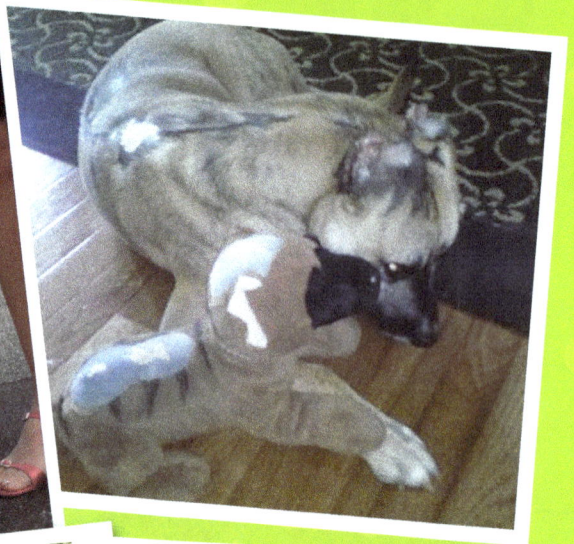

46

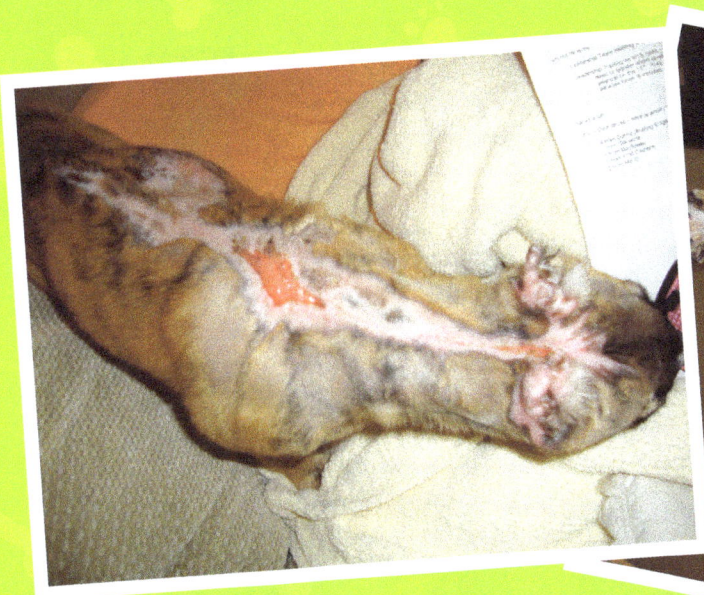
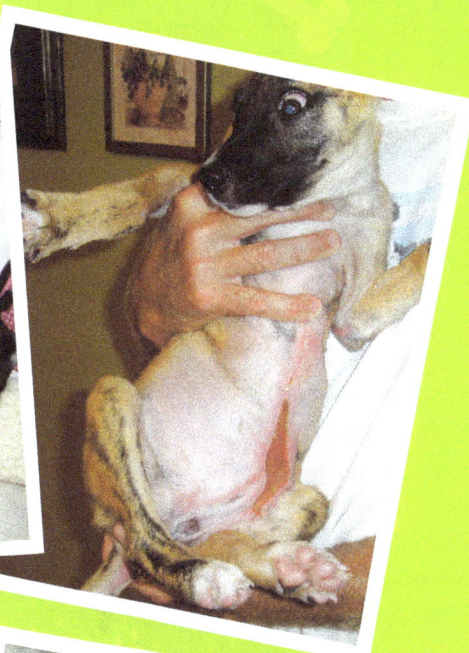

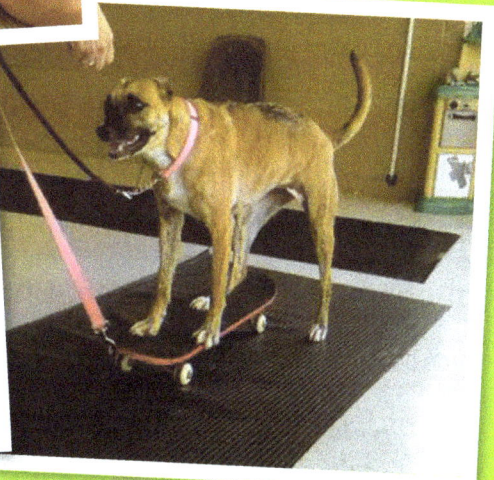

47

Susie's Special Friends
Phoenix and Deborah

Sometimes in life we feel like we live day to day doing the same old things. I had thought about fostering a pet for our animal shelter because I needed more in my life. Then I heard about the puppy that had been burned by four boys. Instantly I had the desire to do something for him. His name is Phoenix.

I agreed to foster him until he was ready for his permanent home. So the journey has begun for many such animals. I had to take him to the Guilford County Animal Shelter for his skin treatments every day seven days a week for seven weeks. This poor puppy had body wraps that had to be removed every day so his wounds could be cleaned. Fridays were much tougher, because the old, dead skin had to be removed. As Phoenix grew, it became harder for him to walk because so much of his skin had been burned that he had had to have skin grafts done.

I watched him sleeping many nights with tears in my eyes. I could tell he was uncomfortable at times. He had to wear a plastic collar for a few months. Sleeping in that collar was no fun. It may have bothered me more than it did him.

He is the most lovable dog, but how can that be? I truly believe that unconditional love and time can heal the physical and emotional wounds and pain of even the most-abused pets. Phoenix is living proof. I have learned so much from him. If he can forgive and love unconditionally, then I can too.

It was a long journey but once again he could hold his head high and life went on. As I share this horrific story with you, my heart is heavy while Phoenix sits gazing at me as if nothing out of the ordinary had ever happened. That's my sweet, loving little man.

~Deborah Hodges

Additional Note: Phoenix was fortunate enough to receive medical care from the shelter through Susie's Miracle Fund.

Susie's Special Friends
Bailey and Keely

Bailey was found on September 9, 2010, walking in a residential area of Greensboro, North Carolina. The people who found him took him to a local veterinarian's office and surrendered him as a "found dog."

The doctors immediately noticed that he was suffering from second- and third-degree burns down his entire back. He was then transported to the Guilford County Animal Shelter and named Bailey by one of the employees.

Bailey was fortunate enough to receive medical care from the shelter through Susie's Miracle Fund.

Around the time when Bailey was located, I read a news story about him on the Internet. The article showed a picture of Bailey and his horrific burns. I remember that he was looking directly at the camera with such a sad, pain-filled expression.

I had already been volunteering with the Susie's Law efforts and at events that raised money for Susie's Miracle Fund. I immediately felt a connection to Bailey and wanted to help him since, at the time, his case was unsolved.

In the mid-1990s, I volunteered with the McDowell County Humane Society. During that time I became a state-certified Animal Cruelty Investigator. I have always had a passion for all animals, especially the broken ones.

I was able to adopt Bailey and bring him home on October 14, 2010. I was told that he was around five years old. It was obvious from that first night that Bailey had been an indoor dog. He was so sweet and completely trusting. I began working on trying to find any information as to where he had come from and what had happened to him.

On April 9, 2011—while at an event benefiting Susie's Miracle Fund—I was told that Bailey's case had been officially closed by the police department. According to their investigation, the people who had originally found Bailey were the actual owners. They stated that Bailey was "accidentally" burned by their mentally handicapped son while he was giving Bailey a bath. The family kept Bailey at home for two days in an attempt to treat him. When they realized that his burns were too significant, they became scared and surrendered Bailey as a found animal. The case was deemed an accident, and no charges were ever pressed.

Bailey is scarred from the middle of his shoulder blades to the base of his tail. His hair will never grow back. He loves to sleep with me at night and begs to go for car rides.

Bailey now accompanies me to various Susie's Hope™ nonprofit organization and Susie's Law events. He is very outgoing, and he loves treats and to be petted. I love to speak to citizens about cruelty to animals, the current laws regarding animals, and how to properly take care of a pet.

Due to Bailey's growing popularity, we created a Facebook page called "Bailey Greene" so that his story could be told.

Today Bailey is my best friend. He currently lives with a pit bull–golden retriever mix and a poodle mix. All three of them are rescued dogs. I believe that Bailey and I have a purpose together in life and we are lucky enough to be able to share our story.

~Keely Greene

The Susie's Hope™ Program Is...

The Susie's Hope™ program features a powerful message of love, hope, and forgiveness.

It's about:

- Facing your fears and watching them disappear.
- Getting a second chance at life and running with it.
- Never giving up hope.
- Loving and trusting again.
- Moving forward and not looking back.
- Living for the moment and not living in the past.
- Not holding on to the negative in life, but focusing on the positive.
- Forgiving those who hurt you and in that way, going from being a victim to being a victor.

—⚊—

Susie and I are on a personal journey to educate and inspire people about the importance of animal safety and animal care. We have been working together as a team to motivate people to love and respect their pets. Education is the best prevention when it comes to animal abuse.

We have been visiting schools, churches, organizations, our special-needs community, pet adoption fairs, and fund-raisers. Soon we hope to visit hospitals and medical facilities to inspire burn victims and cancer patients, along with victims of any kind of violence and abuse.

—⚊—

We tell the story of two miracles—human and animal. Susie and I both survived a brutal attack and lived to tell about it.

~Donna

53

Susie's Hope ™ Pledge

I, _____ , on this _____ day of _____ promise never to abuse, neglect, torture, or bring harm in any way to any kind of animal. I will love and respect all of God's creatures big and small.

To care for my pet, I will provide shelter, water, food, exercise, groomings, and regular checkups. I promise to love and respect my animal and to take care of my pet to the best of my ability.

Hand with paw, I will honor Susie's Law.

_____
Signature

Donna Lawrence
Donna's Signature

_____
Susie's Signature

In Susie's Words

One day a human hurt me really bad.
But to tell you what happened would make you sad.

Instead I will tell you a happy tale
Of all the loving people who made me well.

My friends at the shelter doctored me up
And made me once again a healthy pup.

As I got better, family and friends pitched in
To make sure I was healthy and happy again.

My forever mom, Donna, gave me a home
With unconditional love I had never known.

To keep my animal friends safe, no matter how small,
Hand with paw, Susie's Team and friends changed the law.

A happy ending is what we should share
With all of God's creatures, big and small, everywhere.

So love and respect your pets, and treat them right.
It's time to cuddle up with my mom and say goodnight.

~Susie

Susie's Trainer
Ally Thomas

Working with Donna and Susie has been my pleasure. Donna came to dog school with an open mind and a committed attitude. She wanted to learn how to manage Susie's behavior throughout the new public life that they were about to enter. They started like all of our students with obedience and learning theory. Once they mastered the basics, they moved on to canine acting so that they could entertain the public with tricks, fun skits, and skateboard riding.

I think they were both surprised how interesting and fun learning new things together can be and how much it enhances the bond between human and canine. Susie is one of the most amazing dogs that I have met in my 35-year career. When Susie is at school, she is "just one of the guys," but when it is time to go to work, she does a beautiful job of being the canine advocate for animal rights.

All of us at Southern Tails are so proud of her and Donna.

~Ally

Additional Notes

First Ally Thomas always says that we are the trainers and that she just assists and teaches us to teach our dogs. She has helped me teach Susie many tricks. Ally has assisted me to teach Susie all along the way.

Second Susie has passed the American Kennel Club's Good Canine Citizen certification test. She is certified. This allows her to go into schools and nursing homes.

~Donna

I am Susie. I am a survivor.
I am the voice for all abused and
neglected animals.
Together Donna and I are
spreading the message of love,
hope, and forgiveness.

Susie and I both say to
her abuser,
"You are forgiven."

Instrumental People

Guilford County Animal Shelter staff—Second from left:
Director Marsha Williams

Dr. Ashley Spruill

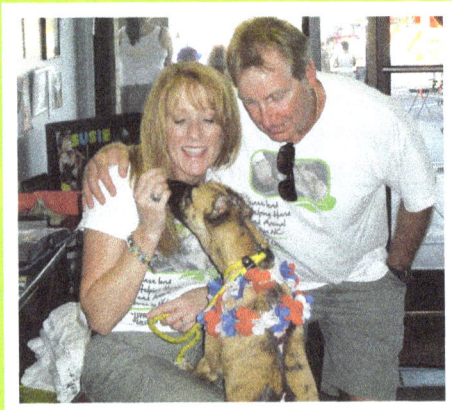

Foster parents Roberta and Bob Wall

Christopher L. Parrish
Assistant District Attorney for the
State of North Carolina in the
18th Prosecutorial District

Susie's Team

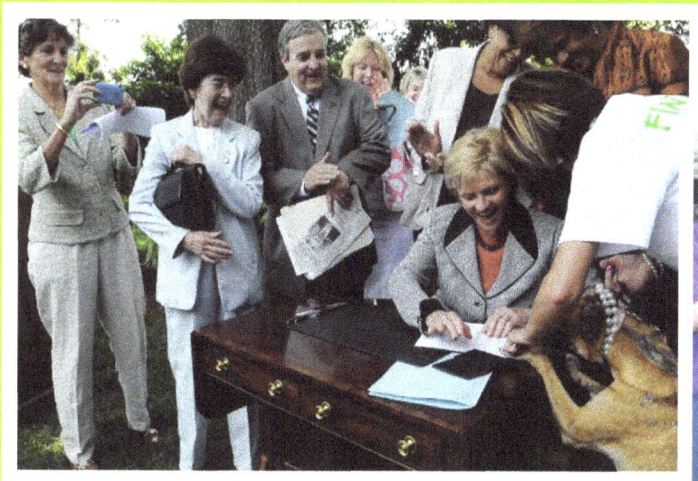

Left to Right: House Representative Pricey Harrison, House Representative Maggie Jeffus, Senator Don Vaughan, *(behind)* House Representative Laura Wiley, House Representative Alma Adams, Governor Bev Perdue, Donna Lawrence, and Susie

Susie's Hope™ Team

The Lawrences: Roy, Baby Girl, Donna, and Susie

61

About the Author and Susie

Donna Lawrence is a native of Pine Hall, North Carolina. She was raised on a farm with her parents and seven brothers and sisters. For 20 years, Donna has been the owner and manager of The Kutting Edge salon in Greensboro.

In October 2008, Donna was attacked by a pit bull and nearly died. Understandably, the attack left her extremely fearful of dogs, but that changed in August 2009. That is when she met Susie, the puppy that had been found beaten, burned, and left to die in a Greensboro, North Carolina, park. Susie has helped Donna overcome her fear of dogs and has given Donna new inspirations for life.

Donna is the Founder and Executive Director of the Susie's Hope™ nonprofit organization that educates children and adults about the importance of animal care and safety.

—⚶—

Susie resides with her mom and dad in High Point, North Carolina. Susie's tragic story became the motivation and inspiration behind Susie's Law that went into effect in North Carolina on December 1, 2010. Susie is a brindle pit bull–shepherd mix. She was adopted by Roy and Donna Lawrence from the Guilford County Animal Shelter on December 8, 2009. The Lawrences have helped Susie learn to love and respect humans who love and respect her.

About the Artist

Jennifer Tipton Cappoen has a bachelor's degree in fine arts from the University of North Carolina at Greensboro. She has spent more than 25 years honing her skills as an illustrator and a designer for both the educational and Christian publishing markets. Her work has been featured in publications by The Education Center, Inc.; New Day Publishing; True Hope Publishing Inc.; Laurus Books; and Bayard Publishing. She lives in Greensboro, North Carolina, with her husband, Andrew, and their four dogs. Their dog Crickett died before we created this book.

www.ingramcontent.com/pod-product-compliance
Lightning Source LLC
Chambersburg PA
CBHW081545040426
42448CB00015B/3234